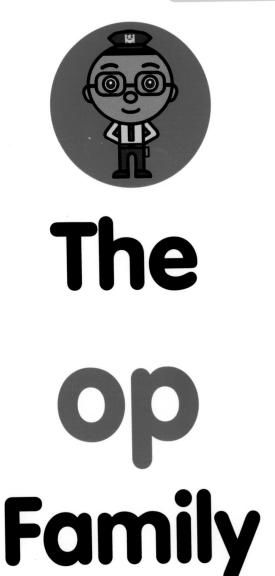

The

op

Family

stop pop

Yukiko Kido

STOP

flip-a

WOR

Word Families

The world is full of print. Written words are everywhere. It's impossible to learn printed words by memorizing them word, by word, by word. To make learning easier, words can be grouped into families.

The words in a word family have two or more letters that are the same. We read "op" words and "un" words, "it" words and "an" words. If you know "op," then it's easier to learn top, pop, and stop.

This book has words from three different word families. All the words in a family rhyme—which means you can add other words to the group by changing the first letter.

It's okay if some of the words you think of are not *real* words. If you make "nop" or "dop" or "zop," it's not wrong— as long as you know the difference between a real word and a nonsense word.

Flip each page and presto-change-o— a new word appears!

pop

cop on top of pop

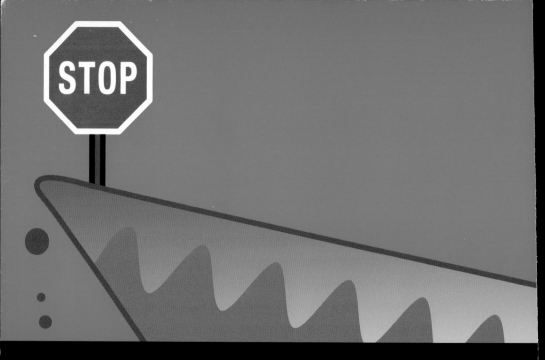

stop on top

top cop

The
un
Family

fun

run bun, run

fun to run

fun in the sun

bun run in the sun

The an Family

man

tan

tan man

tan fan

man with fan

fan on can

The op Family

cop	pop
crop	shop
drop	stop
lop	top

The un Family

bun	run
fun	stun
pun	sun

The an Family

ban	man
bran	pan
can	plan
fan	tan

Find the words in each family.

stop man sun
run bun
tan cop
drop shop can top
stun
man run can drop
stun plan
bran lop
drop pop crop
stop tan
fun cop
pan man
bun lop
ban shop fun
man plan cop sun
tan bran fan
pun top